T0014999

WHO ME?

I'm a
BIOMEDICAL
INFORMATICS EXPERT
now!

prescription. Please con...
dose amount of 200 MCG exceed...
digoxin 50 mcg/...

Common Directions: Prescription s... based...

☐ Free text dosing

☐ Use weight-based dosing formula   10.0

...e:

Dose Unit

Who Me? series co-editors: David A. Weintraub, Professor of Astronomy, of History, and of Communication of Science and Technology, College of Arts & Science, Vanderbilt University; Ann Neely, Professor Emerita of the Practice of Education, Peabody College of Education and Human Development, Vanderbilt University; and Kevin Johnson, Professor of Biomedical Informatics and of Pediatrics, Vanderbilt University Medical Center

Published by

WS Education, an imprint of

World Scientific Publishing Co. Pte. Ltd.

5 Toh Tuck Link, Singapore 596224

USA office: 27 Warren Street, Suite 401-402, Hackensack, NJ 07601

UK office: 57 Shelton Street, Covent Garden, London WC2H 9HE

British Library Cataloguing-in-Publication Data
A catalogue record for this book is available from the British Library.

Who Me? — Vol. 2
I'M A BIOMEDICAL INFORMATICS EXPERT NOW!

ISBN 978-981-124-020-1 (hardcover)
ISBN 978-981-124-021-8 (ebook for institutions)
ISBN 978-981-124-022-5 (ebook for individuals)

Desk Editor: Daniele Lee

Printed in Singapore

P8: megankhines/CC BY-SA 2.0; **P9** (from top down): Sloalan/CC0 1.0, Matt W/CC PDM, Vladislav Litvinov/CC0 1.0, wwarby/CC BY 2.0; **P12**: Sam Howzit/CC BY 2.0; **P14** (from top down): trishhartmann/CC BY 2.0, brian.gratwicke/CC BY 2.0, jpockele/CC BY 2.0, SidPix/CC BY 2.0, USFWS Headquarters/CC PDM 1.0; **P15**: France1978/CC BY-SA 2.0; **P16**: wuestenigel/CC BY 2.0; **P18**: James Michael Morris; **P19**: pingebat (ShutterStock); **P21**: M. Mannell; **P24** (top), **25, 26**: A. Pierce Bounds (Dickinson College class of 1971) and the Archives and Special Collections at Dickinson College, Carlisle PA., USA; **P28**: NEC Corporation of America (Creative Commons license); **P29**: NEC Corporation of America/CC BY 2.0, **P30**: Wikipedia Commons/CC BY 2.0 **P33**: Mia Garchitorena, Vanderbilt University Medical Center, Nashville TN, USA

Who Me?

I'm a BIOMEDICAL INFORMATICS EXPERT now!

Kevin Johnson

Doctor and Biomedical Informatics Expert

Table of contents

Chapter

Kevin in his office at Vanderbilt University Medical Center. Biomedical Informatics researchers work with computers to write software. Kevin uses two screens to make room for all the computer programs he runs. Biomedical Informatics researchers also analyze data and communicate with other scientists using teleconferencing or the phone as a part of their research projects.

1 Discovering Myself

Kevin at age 5

My name is Kevin. I grew up in Baltimore, Maryland. Baltimore is a big and old city, first settled in the year 1659. Baltimore was the home of Francis Scott Key, the author of the "Star-Spangled Banner." Also, Cal Ripken is a famous baseball player who played for the Baltimore Orioles. And Kevin Clash, the voice of Elmo from Sesame Street, is from there! As a child, I knew a lot about famous people from Baltimore, because I was very curious about everything. I always asked lots of questions. I was never afraid to ask things if I did not know the answer. I can even still remember the time I figured out why "afternoon" is called that (because it is after the clock strikes 12:00 p.m.!)

Kevin at age 9

Like a lot of kids, I was always curious about the environment and living things. I was an amateur biologist at the age of seven. My earliest memories involve the outdoors and animals. I especially loved lizards and frogs! Even when we lived in a city neighborhood, I would explore the vacant field behind my house. I would also walk in a nearby park. I would go to these places to play, and I would always discover interesting things there. I found rocks with strange shapes, flowers I didn't recognize, weird bugs, and old coins. Everything I encountered had a story to teach me. I was eager to study the things I found and learn about their stories.

A mason jar terrarium.
This is just like the ones I used to make!

I loved catching lightning bugs (some people call them fireflies). Every summer, when they emerged after dark, I would catch some to watch how they behaved. I would put dirt and rocks at the bottom of a jar and then stick pieces of shrubs into the dirt. I watered it every day. At night the lightning bugs would put on a show. How do they light up? I learned that they didn't light up all the time.

Instead, they only lit up when they were crawling around or flying. In fact, if I made them move by gently shaking the jar, they lit up. This might have been my first experiment! I learned that keeping lightning bugs alive in a jar took a great deal of skill and attention. I loved the challenge of keeping things in my care alive. My first patients were lightning bugs!

After I learned to read, my parents took me to the library so that I could find information that helped me answer my own questions. There, I found books in which I could learn about new things. I also met other people who would sometimes help me find answers to my questions about harder subjects. I was never shy about politely asking questions.

One day, my parents and I visited my older sister's school. There, just outside the principal's office, was a terrarium. Inside were two green lizards with red flaps of skin under their mouths, and a few crickets for them to eat. I was mesmerized. The teacher called these lizards chameleons. The next day, I went to the library and borrowed books so I could read about chameleons. I learned that the right name for them is "anoles." By reading books, I became an anole "expert" at the age of five!

Anole "expert"

The top two pictures are of the same anole, and the bottom two pictures are of the same chameleon. What do they have in common? They change color! That's why people call anoles chameleons. In informatics and medicine, accuracy is important.

Understanding the scientific names of animals was important training for me.

My parents lived in a neighborhood outside the city of Baltimore. Some of the kids in my neighborhood liked the same things I did. We played in the fields and ran to the ice cream truck together, and we never fought. But my grandmother lived in a different part of Baltimore where there were big buildings, more crime, and less green spaces. When I visited my grandmother, we weren't allowed to go exploring. It wasn't safe. And unlike at home, the other kids there had nothing in common with me. There were no parks where they lived, so they had less exposure to nature and didn't want to explore the world the way I did.

During my summers with my grandmother, I had to play in her small backyard with the big tulip tree, or in the nearby alley. I climbed that tree SO many times!

Here is where I learned another thing about myself. Sometimes I felt like an oddball around other kids my age, and that was OK! I was even teased because I didn't speak like them or dress like them. Some of the older kids bullied me because I was different. Luckily, my relatives saw what was happening and talked to me about it. They taught me to appreciate myself, even when kids in the neighborhood treated me badly. I learned to be strong and confident in myself. That lesson has helped me for my entire life, as you will see.

I remember hearing the song "Supercalifragilisticexpialidocious" from the movie *Mary Poppins*. I learned how to say that made-up word, which was fun to do. In the movie, they even said that word backwards. Saying the word backwards — dociousaliexpiesticfragicalirupus — was hard.

Also, saying a word backwards didn't make sense to me. I spent lots of time thinking about backwards words. Even after thinking hard, I couldn't figure out why the grown-ups in the movie had said that. I asked some of the kids I played with in my grandmother's neighborhood if they knew why. I can still remember how strangely they looked at me when I first said supercalifragilisticexpialidocious and then said it backwards, too. The next thing I knew, other kids were coming to my yard asking me to say those words.

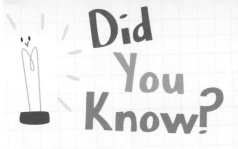

Did You Know?

Did you notice that dociousaliexpiesticfragicalirupus is not really Supercalifragilisticexpialidocious backwards? They tricked us in that movie!

Have you heard of a palindrome? That is the name for words that read the same backward and forward (like mom, noon, or racecar. Do you know any other palindromes?)

Each of these vessels is a K_YA_. Can you fill in the letters to this palindrome?

_____

Here is a picture from *Mary Poppins*. I loved musicals from an early age. This one is funny for kids, but has a serious message for grown-ups.

The first house I lived in was in the city, and is the picture on the left. The second house I lived in, in the suburbs, is on the right.

When I turned eight, my family moved out of the city to the suburbs outside Baltimore. Going to a new school was hard because I didn't know anyone there. I became less comfortable asking questions out loud. I also had a hard time making friends with new classmates. I felt much more at ease asking my questions to adults outside of school hours. I wish I had not stopped asking questions at school, because it made school less fun for a while.

My parents knew this move was hard for me and my siblings. To help us, we got a pet dog I named Lucky. I don't remember why I named him Lucky, but I think it might have been because of how lucky we both were to find each other.

Mr. Joe was a neighbor who lived across the street. He was a friendly man who also had a dog. My dog Lucky and his dog liked to play together in the backyard. Eventually, with my parents' approval, I was allowed to join Mr. Joe and his dog on weekly walks. The four of us started walking on nearby nature trails. We used our powers of observation to explore along the way. We saw caterpillars, plants that grew out of dead logs, and all sorts of rocks. Now, I had even more reading to do so I could learn about all these things! Books and magazines from the library taught me about monarch butterflies (my favorite kind of butterfly) and cicadas.

Frogs, salamanders and newts begin life as tadpoles that live in ponds and streams!

Cicadas begin life as beetles that live underground.

How does a caterpillar become a butterfly? Answer: It lives in a chrysalis for a few weeks. While it is in there, it grows wings and changes into a butterfly.

These animals all look different as babies than they do as adults. Why does this happen? Animals that change when they become adults are undergoing **metamorphosis**. Scientists think that animals evolved this way so that babies do not compete for the same food as their parents. Parents and babies also inhabit different environments. Living in different environments makes it easier for the species to survive. How do people answer these questions? They do research, analyze data and make comparisons between different animals. This is an important way in which science moves forward.

That Christmas, Santa gave me an amazing gift. It was called an erector set. An erector set contained small pieces of metal, screws, a motor and wheels, along with an instruction book that explained how to make buildings, cars, and bridges. In no time, I had constructed everything in the instruction book. That is when I learned another important lesson. I am very creative! I made all sorts of things with my erector set. I even built a small, working radio and a robot. I was a budding engineer!

My parents and friends were amazed by my creativity. I loved imagining the things I could make using my brain and a few tools. But most importantly, I had discovered an important aspect of who I was.

So what does a curious kid, who is interested in caring for living things, and loves to be creative, do? The answer to that became obvious to me by the time I was 13.

An advertisement for an erector set, very similar to the one I received when I was young.

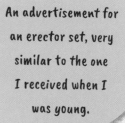

15

2 Becoming a Scientist

In school, I became interested in doing experiments. Before I started school, my questions were all "Why" questions. Why do lizards change colors? Why do frogs start out as tadpoles? Those questions made sense when I was observing and learning about things in the world around me.

In elementary school, I learned to ask a new kind of question that leads directly to science experiments: "What happens if ___?" These new questions challenged me to wonder not just about how things were, but about what happens when things change, or when I tried to make changes happen.

I was doing experiments all the time. One time, I grew a pineapple plant by planting the top of a pineapple my parents had bought in the grocery store. In another store, I saw a white rock that sparkled. I asked the store owner about that rock. He said it was made of a mineral called quartz, which is the most abundant mineral in rocks found on the surface of the Earth. He told me that the internal structure of the atoms in quartz rock is a crystal, just like sugar. He told me about a neat experiment I could do at home to create my own crystal. I went home and did what the storekeeper told me. I mixed together sugar and hot water in a jar. Then, I used a popsicle stick to suspend a string in the mixture. One week later, I had rock candy!

What is a crystal, you ask? It looks like a piece of rock. But at the microscopic level, its atoms are arranged in a specific, repeating pattern. Here's how you make a crystal.

Crystal (rock candy) recipe

You only need a few common kitchen materials for this crystal project:

▶ 3 cups sugar

▶ 1 cup boiling water

▶ wooden skewer or cotton string

1 Ask an adult to boil the water in a pot.

2 Add the sugar to the boiling water. Stir it until you don't see any sugar in the water or on the bottom. You can heat the sugar solution on the stove or in the microwave oven if you have trouble getting the sugar to dissolve.

3 Let the water cool a bit before pouring it into your jar, because some jars will break if you pour boiling water into them.

4 Pour the sugar solution into a jar. Place a wooden skewer into the jar or else hang a string into the middle of the jar, tied to a pencil or butter knife.

5 Place the container somewhere where it won't be disturbed. You may wish to cover the jar with a napkin or paper towel to allow evaporation while keeping the crystal solution clean.

6 It may take a few days to get good crystal growth. If you see crystals forming on the top of the jar, you can remove them and eat them. If you leave them, these crystals will compete with your stick or string for sugar and will reduce the size of your crystals.

7 Remove the crystals and enjoy them! If you want to store the crystals before eating them, keep them in an airtight container so that humidity in the air won't make the rock candy sticky.

8 Write down what you observe every day. When you are done, take a picture of your crystal. Eat some. How does it taste? How long did it take to grow your crystal? You just did a science experiment! If you tried to grow one inside and one outside, which would finish first? Why?

My love of science took off in middle school. One day when I was in a pet store, I saw a very rare and very dead lizard in a tank. It was a golden tegu. I knew that these lizards drank water only from leaves. The store manager did not know this. He had given the lizard water in a bowl. That is why the lizard died. Many rare animals found in pet stores die before they ever find new homes. I realized that these animals were being killed by people who lacked experience caring for them properly. Experienced owners use quality improvement techniques to learn from what they observe from animal behavior and make changes that make animals healthier. (Sounds like what doctors do with people, doesn't it?)

I had heard that goldfish could be stored by freezing them for short periods in liquid nitrogen. Then they could be warmed up and revived. I thought, "Why not do that for rare animals and fish?" I did a science experiment with liquid nitrogen. I froze a goldfish and an African frog. The goldfish survived, but the frog was injured. I reported this at our local science fair and won an award! I had fun talking to people about my ideas and showing them my experiments. I knew then that I wanted to pursue science for my career.

Did You Know?

Quality Improvement in Informatics

Even the most well-trained people are still human and commit human error. There are many reasons why computers might be able to do some tasks better than people.

Look at the nine items in the boxes below. Do people sometimes have any of these problems? Do computers?

Tired	Doing two things at once	Forgetful
Afraid	Biased	Ill
Unable	Bored	Unavailable

3 Becoming a Doctor

My walks with Mr. Joe had a huge impact on me. They helped me realize how I could combine my love of science with my interest in taking care of animals. One day, I found a baby crawfish in a stream and took it home. I set up a little aquarium and kept it and watched it grow. Raising animals meant learning about how they lived in the wild and paying attention to details about their eating and sleeping habits. Often, animals get sick and need to be nursed back to good health, just like people. By the time I was in middle school, I always had some sort of pet I was raising or trying to breed.

When I was in middle school, I fell in love with tropical fish. I became a regular visitor to the local pet store. I convinced my parents to let me spend some of the money I was earning from my dog-walking job to buy and set up fish tanks with tropical fish. I started with molly fish and angelfish, but soon fell in love with cichlids. Cichlids are a type of fish found all over the world. They are harder to keep than many other fish, but fun to watch because cichlid parents take care of their babies. Not all tropical fish do that. For example, the cichlid parents make a nest, just like birds do. Then they take turns watching their offspring. In some cases, the

Look closely in the mouth of this pet cichlid
(Labidochromis caeruleus).
What do you see?

babies even live inside the mouths of their parents until they are old enough to swim out! To breed cichlids, the conditions in the aquarium must be just like those in nature. For example, lights must come on and go off at the same time every day. I decided to use timers to automate the lights. I was able to breed many species of cichlids, after I learned how to simulate their natural environment. I raised their offspring and sold them to pet stores for more money. Sometimes, I exchanged them for even rarer and more expensive fish.

A green gecko from Madagascar.

I also loved lizards and started collecting them when I was in junior high school. I kept more than 12 different species as pets. My favorite lizards are called geckos. They are entertaining in a lot of ways. They are able to climb on walls without claws because their feet are covered with hundreds of tiny hairs that can stick to the walls. They use their tongues to lick their eyes. Some even have voices! And many are very colorful.

After I got more skilled at studying animals and learning how to care for them, I decided to get the oddest sea creature of all, an octopus! My pet octopus taught me a lot about the importance of paying attention to details. I had to keep the temperature and salinity level of the salt water in a very specific range for the octopus to be happy and healthy. I kept a logbook and learned to interpret data to know what to do each week. I also had to automate the lights, the heater, and even one of the filters to keep the water quality high. I became very skilled at taking care of the octopus.

I decided to combine my interests in science and animals. Over the years, I took many pets to see a doctor who takes care of animals, a veterinarian, when they were sick. What a fun job that could be! I dreamed that I would grow up to be a veterinarian. I knew that college was the first step to becoming a scientist and a veterinarian. I was excited about taking that first step and going to college. I chose Dickinson College in Pennsylvania.

Dickinson College is a liberal arts school. Liberal arts schools require students to study history, literature, writing, philosophy, sociology, psychology, science, creative arts and more. Students who earn a liberal arts degree learn to formulate effective arguments, to communicate well and solve problems. Dickinson College was a great school for a curious person like me who wanted to be taught by teachers who loved curiosity.

Me visiting New York City. College allowed me to travel and see new parts of the country. Scientists and physicians need to become comfortable meeting people from different communities. Through friends in college, I became more aware of how other people lived. I also had a lot of fun!

When I started college, I lacked confidence. I didn't think I belonged at college. I was one of only a few Black students there. Because most other students at my college didn't look like me, I was uncomfortable at first. I even thought all the other students were smarter than me. But I worked hard. I kept going to class. I learned French (J'aime apprendre!). I kept doing my homework.

I slowly learned something very important: Coming from public schools meant I had more to learn but I could do as well in my classes as the other students if I tried hard enough.

I did belong in college!

That's me!

I discovered that college was also a time and place for doing lots of other things in addition to my classwork. I played sports like tennis, racquetball and track, but my favorite activity was music. I found three ways to enjoy music: I played music on the local radio station. I sang in a choir and played bass in the orchestra. I even acted and sang in musicals!

This is me (t from the rig performing musical in co

It turns out that many top scientists also enjoy sports and music. I had learnt about Dr. Charles Drew, the physician, scientist, athlete and musician who developed the techniques to store blood. He looked like me and became a role model for me. I also worked with a veterinarian named Dr. Rill for the first two years of college. I learned a lot about being a veterinarian. It was fun, but it was different from just having pets. Something was missing.

Dr. Charles Drew

I was on my way to becoming a veterinarian when something very sad but important happened. During my junior year of college, a good friend of mine became sick. My friends and I had to rush him to the emergency department. He was diagnosed with a serious disease. His parents took him back home to Baltimore. I visited him in the hospital over our winter break. As he got better, I realized how important science was in helping doctors know how to properly care for him. They had to figure out what was wrong before they could help him get better. Interviewing his family provided important clues. Then they had to decide on the best therapy, from hundreds of possible medications. When one medication didn't work, they switched to another medication. Eventually, he got better and was discharged from hospital.

Hospitals are not just where sick people become well. Hospitals are where scientists work. Doctors are scientists who take care of people. Even though I loved animals, I realized that doctors had to be curious and had to be able to teach, so that people could learn how to stay healthy. I saw doctors doing more teaching than veterinarians. I also saw that asking questions and being able to answer them were required of good doctor scientists. It sounded like the perfect job for me. I was hooked.

TENNIS

The 1980 Men's Tennis Team, led by sophomore captain Steve Rockoff, turned out a 500 season. The team played some tough competition this year, but because this was their first year together, they expect a much improved season next year. The same team will return with a lot more dedication and experience. The Men's Tennis Team will continue its winning ways to be a team of which the school

This is me playing tennis for my college tennis team.

I loved college so much that I studied very hard in my classes and got involved in research at a science laboratory. Because of these two things, I graduated with honors. I also received an award when I graduated for being an outstanding graduating senior. My parents were there to see me win the award, and they were very proud.

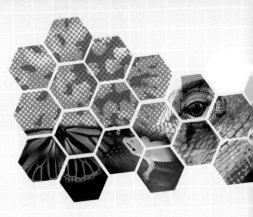

I received the award for outstanding graduating senior in college. My parents were there to see me get this. It was a highlight of my time in college. The President of the college, President Banks, is shown here congratulating me. We knew each other and had become friends.

4 Becoming a Biomedical Informatics Doctor

In college, I learned about all types of science. I also discovered computer programming, which I really enjoyed. Writing the instructions to make a computer do the things I wanted it to do was like using the erector set. I could dream up an idea for solving a problem. Then I could solve it by programming the computer!

I now love computers and the powerful things they can do with data. I realized that computers were the library of the future. Working with Dr. Rill, I realized how much doctors had to know. To take care of patients, doctors must record and process a lot of data. Dr. Rill sometimes went back to his office to learn things before seeing an animal patient.

[Chart] [StNotes] [Forms] [Panels] [Pt.Lists] [TaskList] [MsgBskts] [WhBoards] [NewRes] [SignDrafts] [Misc.]

[-] [1] [2] [3]

3700834 **ZTEST, ARTT** (12/08/1939 - 81YO M) (615) 867-5309 P H POST: Yes Alert Deceased Sec.Risk **PCP:** Hock, Richard Lloyd
lDocuments Apptm. EnterData Faxed Flows FastLabs Labs Meds Msgs? Reminders? Orders Pt.summary Search AddToPanel VitalSigns DCINoDo
muniz. TeamSummary UploadImage Who documented?

/18/17	♦WIC Outpatient Forms (English)	Peterson, Anna J
	♦Communication and Consent Authorization	10/18/17 16:06
/17/17	♦IV - Peripheral Insertion Flowsheet	Grande, Jonathan F
/14/17	♦Outside Facility Order Requisition	10/14/17
	♦**Orders:** Outpatient	Albert, Dan W
/13/17	♦Outside Facility Order Requisition	10/13/17
	♦Outside Facility Order Requisition	10/13/17

023700834 ZTEST, ARTT (12/08/1939 - 81YO M) Alert Deceased Sec.Risk **Research Participant**

Print   Custo

atient-specific guidelines   MedicationsLog
                                              ICD9/10 History

Please place a Transitional Care Consult order if the patient is to be admitted.

Structured Problems: (10/06/17 09:13, Karki, Kanchan for _Voom_	Adverse and Allergic Drug Reactions: (10/06/17 09:13, Karki, Kanchan for _Voom_
esource)	iodine (hives)
Glaucoma	zinc sulfate (hives)
Gastroesophageal reflux disease	barium sulfate (vomiting) [dx: 09/18/2017]
Acne	**Medications:** prepare to print print and give pt. Show Hx of medica
Possible pregnancy [dx: 09/18/2017]	_eStar)_
Plague unspecified [2<5 Chipmunks & Squirrels]	acetaminophen-codeine (TYLENOL #2) 300-15 mg per tablet: Take 1 tablet by mo
troke	budesonide (PULMICORT) 0.5 mg/2 mL nebulizer solution: (Also Known As Pulm
	cycloSPORINE (RESTASIS) 0.05 % ophthalmic emulsion: Administer 1 drop into
	ERGOCALCIFEROL, VITAMIN D2, ORAL: 1000mg, BID, po, 30 days
	fluticasone-salmeterol (ADVAIR DISKUS) 250-50 mcg/dose diskus inhaler: Inhale
	morning and evening.
	HYDRALAZINE HCL (HYDRALAZINE ORAL): 75 mg tablet by mouth every 8
	levothyroxine (SYNTHROID) 100 mcg tablet: 0.25 tablet by mouth daily for 6 mo
	lisinopril (PRINIVIL,ZESTRIL) 2.5 mg tablet: Take 1 tablet by mouth daily.
	MESALAMINE (ASACOL ORAL): 1600 mg (4 400 mg capsules) daily
	metoprolol su-hydrochlorothiaz 100-12.5 mg tablet extended release 24 hr: Take 1
	metoprolol tartrate (LOPRESSOR) 100 mg tablet: Take 1 tablet by mouth daily.
	nortriptyline (PAMELOR) 75 mg capsule: Take 1 capsule by mouth daily.
	pantoprazole (PROTONIX) 40 mg EC tablet: Take 1 tablet by mouth daily.
	timolol (BETIMOL) 0.5 % ophthalmic solution: Administer 1 drop into both eyes

Here is an example of the enormous amount
of information in a medical record for
one patient. Note all the tabs at the top.
Everything that is not black can be clicked.
Every click brings up more information.

/Herb Interactions *(06/25/19 00:44,*

eded for pain. For one time only.
r (0.25 mg) irrigation twice a day
) times a day. For 6 months.

(twelve) hours. 2 times per day

daily. For 90 day(s).

ay.

Doctors also must remember every possible disease that could match a patient's **symptoms** and measurements. All that remembering is very hard. Even the smartest doctors can't remember everything. I realized that doctors could get help from computers, because computers can remember things better than human brains can.

Computers can do a better job than doctors in storing information about patients and knowing about different kinds of diseases. I wondered if having a computer in the office would make learning on the job easier. I began to wonder if computers could help doctors help sick people in other ways. Could a computer suggest the diagnosis? Could patients use computers to diagnose themselves and thus avoid going to the doctor?

As usual, I read books to find answers to my questions and found out about the existence of a scientific specialty called **biomedical informatics**. Biomedical informatics doctors combine knowledge about computer science, medicine and biology to help doctors store and retrieve and learn new things with information. It was a new field (computers were new way back in the 1970s!), but had the potential to fix lots of problems in healthcare. I knew that doing these things would take many years. That's when I decided I would spend the rest of my life working as a biomedical informatics doctor, making my dream for helping other doctors come true.

What are some of the data doctors must track?

- Some diseases cause fevers, so doctors measure temperatures of healthy and sick patients. The temperature of their patient is one kind of data a doctor must track.

- A person's weight is important for prescribing the right amount of needed medicine. So, doctors and nurses also measure how much people weigh. Weight is a second kind of data about their patients that doctors must track.

- High blood pressure is very dangerous. It can cause heart attacks and strokes and damage other organs, like the kidneys. Doctors and nurses always measure the blood pressure of their patients and treat a person with abnormally high blood pressure with medication. Blood pressure is a third kind of patient data that a doctor must track.

After finishing college, I applied to over 15 medical schools. I was fortunate to be accepted to Johns Hopkins School of Medicine, which is one of the best medical schools in the world. At Hopkins, I learned about many fields of medicine. I could become whatever kind of doctor I wanted. I decided to become a pediatrician — a doctor who takes care of children. Children remind me of myself. They are curious and love to ask questions.

They see the world and use their brains to make sense of what they observe. But many of them learn to stop being inquisitive. I was determined to be a doctor my young patients could see as a role model. I often reminded parents, "Children are small, but not stupid!" Friends also remind me that newborn children are like my pets, because they don't communicate using words. For that reason, my decision to become a pediatrician seemed natural to them!

For many years, I worked as both a pediatrician and a biomedical informatics doctor. Over time, my work in informatics and helping other doctors required all of my time. I no longer had time to work directly with patients. I still love being a doctor, but now, by using computers, I take care of thousands of patients instead of just a few.

Me listening to the heart and lungs of a patient.

5 Making a Difference in Medicine

As a pediatrician who specializes in biomedical informatics, I ask questions about how to improve the way doctors care for patients. Then I come up with experiments that use computers to see how computer programs can help doctors take even better care of their patients. I make sure these computers store all the medical measurements doctors make of their patients. I also help the doctors use the data from lots of patients to discover patterns. These patterns can help doctors cure diseases.

How many facts can you remember at one time? Most people can remember seven things at one time. But not more than seven. Seven is called the Magic Number, and it has to do with the limits of our brains.

Try it. Memorize these words and then close your eyes and list them.

- Feather
- Train
- Onion
- Travel
- Mailbox
- Apple
- Blue
- Pencil
- Gardener
- Fire

How many did you get right? Did you remember more than five? How about more than seven? Did you remember them all? Most adults can remember between five and seven items on a list. A few exceptional people can remember nine or more things.

This picture shows all the data that goes into a computer working with doctors. How many types of data do you see?

In healthcare today, a doctor might have to use 20 or more facts in order to decide what and how much medication to give a patient! Carefully sorting through so much data and always getting the very best answer is almost impossible, even for the most experienced and careful doctor. This is why computers are so important. Computers have no limit to the number of facts they can remember. Computers can juggle all these facts and then sort through them to make recommendations to the doctor. Advice from computers can help doctors make the best decision for each patient.

Computers need to retain facts. Computers also need to understand data and answer questions. Facts come in different forms. Some facts are about a person's body, like age, weight, temperature and blood pressure. Other facts are about different kinds of diseases. For example, a person with chicken pox likely has a rash with blisters and scabs; in comparison, a person with pink eye would have very different symptoms, like red and itchy eyes and a yellow crust that forms on the eyelashes. Side effects a patient may have had from medication they took in the past are also important.

Doctors even know some facts about which medication works best for patients who have genes like yours! All these facts have to be stored in the computer. When a doctor asks the computer for help, all these facts have to be easy to find. Then the computer can respond quickly and offer advice that will help the doctor make good decisions about how to care for the patient.

The big problem I'm trying to solve now is about finding the best medicine to use to help each patient. We use three kinds of data to do this: Data about the patient's symptoms, his genes, and what medicine has not helped him before. With that combination of data, the computers can help the doctors decide on the best medicine to prescribe for that patient. The hospital where I work, Vanderbilt University Medical Center, has used this system for ten years. And I've been working on finding better and better solutions to this problem for 25 years! Every year, the computers do a better job because I help improve the way they use data.

How does a computer help the doctor? First it must have information about the patient that might help make sure a decision is the right one. Then the computer asks questions to itself! In some cases, if the answer causes concern, the computer alerts the doctor.

Finding the best medicine for a sick person may sound easy to do, but it is not. Sometimes, a sick person does not use the right words to describe the ways in which they are sick. They do not do this on purpose. Doctors use different, more exact words than other people to describe the same problem. Parents often use different words than children. A parent might say that their child has a fever, while the child may say "I'm cold" or "I don't feel good." Very young children might not use words at all! The words we use are vital in helping diagnose illnesses. But with so many different words, identifying a disease and picking the right medicine can be difficult. Just like finding a needle in a haystack, solving this problem is very hard, but not impossible. One goal of my work in biomedical informatics is to find the right, most important words and help computers use them to improve healthcare.

This is an image from a program I wrote to help children remember to take their medication. It runs on a phone, which was one of the first programs of its kind in the world. The concept has now been added to many other programs that run on phones around the world.

I created a computer program to help people remember to take their medicine. Patients with diseases like asthma and diabetes often forget to take their medication at the right time. Often, they forget to take them at all. They are most likely to forget to take any new medication the doctor prescribes for them. Some patients with severe diseases, like cystic fibrosis, can be very sick if they forget to take their medication. What if a computer could remind them? What if a computer could send a message to someone else with a reminder to remind their friend or brother? I helped develop a system to send text messages to patients when it was time to take their medicine. Even children as young as 7 years old can use this system! If the patient doesn't answer the message, the computer sends another message to a friend or a member of their family. That person can help remind them to take their medicine. This reminder system works very well. Now companies around the world use this idea. One very important problem in hospitals is that doctors and patients don't always control what happens in healthcare. Sometimes the government changes how they work with hospitals. I have discovered how to use movies about informatics to help the people who work in hospitals adjust to big changes.

I learned through my love of science and animals that I was very creative. I use my creativity to write stories about problems in medicine. I use music, pictures, and interviews to tell stories through documentary movies. I have now made two documentaries. They have been seen by more than 30,000 people. One was even shown at a national film festival!

All of the work I have done to improve healthcare has been fun and rewarding. Because of my work, I won a national award. My parents and sisters were even in the audience!

I have been the first to do a lot of things. I was the first one in my family to become a doctor. I was the first Black student at my college to win the most outstanding senior award. I was the first Black person to be named the head pediatric resident at Johns Hopkins University. I was even the first Black faculty physician at Vanderbilt University Medical Center to be promoted to tenured professor.

This is a picture from my film, "No Matter Where." The film uses animation to help explain challenging concepts.

I plan to continue to invent new ways that computers can help doctors and patients. I'm a successful pediatrician, scientist, athlete and teacher. I continue to be curious, to take care of animals and to experiment in all aspects of my life.

NATIONAL ACADEMY OF MEDICINE

IN RECOGNITION OF OUTSTANDING CONTRIBUTIONS TO THE FIELD OF HEALTH

KEVIN B. JOHNSON

WAS ELECTED A MEMBER OF THE NATIONAL ACADEMY OF MEDICINE
(FORMERLY THE INSTITUTE OF MEDICINE)

OCTOBER 1, 2010

HOME SECRETARY   PRESIDENT   FOREIGN SECRETARY

My official certificate of membership into the Institute of Medicine, now called the National Academy of Medicine. Many of the best scientists in the country are members. It was the honor of my life to receive this award!

I have one more key lesson to share: I didn't become a biomedical informatics expert all by myself. No one can be successful in school or in their career without help. Hundreds of people helped pave the way for me, and dozens more encouraged and helped me personally to succeed. I had relatives who supported me. They were kind and encouraged me when some others didn't. There were adults who "got" me. There were places, like libraries and pet shops, where I could go to fuel my passion for learning and trying new things.

Believe it or not, when I was young, the Internet did not exist yet. There was no way to learn about people who lived far away from where I lived. You have opportunities to do that today. There is a way for each of you to discover who you are, what you love, and what good you will do for the world. You just have to be courageous and confident.

Me attending a scientific meeting with fellow scientists and physicians (top left). My family (top right). The members of my last clinic at Johns Hopkins (bottom left). My parents and me with my daughter Natalie at her high school graduation (bottom right).

38

GLOSSARY

Asthma
A condition in which a person has difficulty breathing.

Biomedical informatics
A scientific field (like computer science or biology) that studies how data (like your age, your medical problems, your genes, or your street address) can be used to improve your health and the way doctors and nurses work.

Chameleons
Small lizards that can change the color of their skin.

Diabetes
A disease in which a person's body does not process food properly to make energy.

Genes
A part of every cell in your body that tells it how to work. Who you are and what you look like is mostly based on your genes.

Metamorphosis
A major change in the shape or look of an animal as it matures.

Natural environment
Everything that exists in the world around us that is not made by humans.

Palindrome
A word or phrase that is spelled the same backward and forward.

Pediatrician
A doctor who takes care of children.

Salinity
The amount of salt dissolved in water.

Symptoms
A physical problem, like a headache or tiredness, that may indicate that a person is sick.

Terrarium
A container with glass sides for growing plants and small animals indoors.

Discussion Questions

1. What do you think Dr. Johnson's relatives told him when he said he felt like an outsider in his grandmother's neighborhood?

2. Do you have a "Mr. Joe" in your life? Who or what has helped you learn about yourself?

3. Biomedical informatics helps doctors every day. What are some of the things your doctor has done that you think he uses his memory for? How could a computer help your doctor?

4. Dr. Johnson uses his creativity to solve lots of problems in informatics. Use your creativity to solve this problem:

   A patient comes to see the doctor with an unusual set of findings. The doctor remembers she saw another patient with these findings last year and runs some tests. This patient has the same disease. The doctor thinks to herself, "Every patient with an unusual set of findings is probably like another patient somewhere in the world. I wonder how we could use this information to help other doctors diagnose all these other patients!"

   Describe how we could do this. Hint: there's always the Internet and the smartphone.

Additional Resources

More information about Dr. Kevin Johnson can be found at
http://www.kevinbjohnsonmd.net
More information about biomedical informatics can be found at:
https://www.amia.org/why-informatics
More information about Dr. Charles Drew can be found at:
https://www.acs.org/content/acs/en/education/whatischemistry/
african-americans-in-sciences/charles-richard-drew.html